Write Your Way Out: If Not Now, When?

Divine Principles For Planning, Proclaiming, and Pursing your Purpose with Purpose.

Corey R. Washington Sr.

Contents

Dedication	1
Acknowledgments	3
Introduction	7
Prelude	11
1. Write The Vision and Make it Plain	13
2. Write Your Way Out	21
3. The Writing Is On The Wall	31
4. The Significance Of the Hand and Writing	39
5. The Writing Cannot Be Interpreted	45
6. What is Written Must Come to Pass	51
7. Your Testimony Is The Treasure That Connects You To Your Vision: Reach Back Into Your Treasure Chest	57
8. Vision Materialized: New Beginnings	65
References and Citations	69

Dedication

I dedicate this book to the memory of my dear mother, **Regina Marie Washington,** *who I promised while holding her hand as she took her last breath in 2006 that I would make something of myself and make her proud. This is the first of many works and accomplishments in the Lord and in the power of his might, mama! I dedicate this book to the memory of my "earthly" father,* **Robert Lee Grady,**" *and as a byproduct of them both, I also dedicate and pass on this book to my sons* **Corey Jr***,* **Joshua***, and* **Jeremiah** *as a road-map, guideline, and even encouragement in times when they feel as if their dreams are out of reach and impossible. The possibilities of your present don't have to be predicated upon your past! All things are possible with God! All things are possible to him who believes! You are not defined by your past or by the levels and limitations of your parents but rather what you do with your present!* **Your choices determine the course of your life!**

Acknowledgments

First and foremost, I give all praise, honor, and glory to God the Father, **God the Son, and God the Holy Spirit** for all the insight and revelation that he provided me as my helper, advocate, standby and guide. Truly, I am only able to write because of his empowerment and presence. I thank him for keeping me and knowing me even before I entered my mother's womb! Through the good, the bad, and the ugly, "He was there all the time!"

Jamal Washington, My one and only brother from the same mother, "Am I my brother's keeper?" "Yes, I Am." We are the Legacy!

Minister Robert Williams, who I sought one night like "Nicodemus," seeking out the savior who led me to the Lord back in 1995. Besides receiving the precious Holy Spirit, this has been one of the greatest gifts that I have ever received.

Pastor Percy E. Hughes & Missionary Ruby Scott of the "Bronx Church of God In Christ" where I was offered Christ as I walked down the aisle and received the greatest gift ever! I received salvation and his gift of the precious Holy Spirit!

Pastor Mother C.E. Frasier of the "Number one House of Deliverance and Prayer for all people" where I experienced firsthand the love of God in demonstration according to the biblical pattern of, "These signs shall follow them that believe." I am still being led and guided by many of her teachings that sparked my curiosity into who I am in Christ. I sincerely and effectually carry her with me still to this day!

Apostle Ernest Leonard of the "Provision of Promise

Ministries" where I attended "The School of the Holy Spirit" where the "Apostolic" and the "Prophetic" began to truly reveal what was on the inside of me. There I realized, as he would often say, "I didn't have to take the Devil's junk because Jesus Christ is Lord!"

Pastor Amos F. Kemper III of "St. Samuel Cathedral Church of God in Christ who offered me "the right hand of fellowship" and a place on his pulpit and Ministerial board. It is and has been, one of the biggest Honors in Ministry for me as this giant in the faith and pioneer is known around the world as a man of Prayer, Fasting, Signs, Wonders, and Miracles with a keen spirit of "Discernment." It warms my heart and strengthens my spirit to know that he is yet praying for me today!

Evangelist Sheria Stallings of St. Samuel Cathedral Church of God In Christ **(AKA Cheerleader for Christ)**, whose "tremendous faith" has seen things that I could not see in myself. She has truly helped me to see that "there are more on my side than against me because I have the Lord of Host fighting for me with one simple prayer:

"Open his eyes Lord so that he may see." Her continued perspective on "seeing the glass half full as opposed to seeing it half empty" has helped change my perception of life from that of "merely living and existing" to "soaring, thriving, and living life more "abundantly" from the inside out! She is truly the anchor and rock that holds her family together!

The following **"Divine Connections"** have proven to be the bridges that continue to carry me over and through at present:

Reverend Gail Richardson and the Honey Gurls Ministries.

Open Bible Church International, where Bishop Francois & Dr. Kimala, along with Elder Garner, allowed me to "break bread" while stirring up the gifts that were inside me.

Deacon/Elder Lofton and family of "Open Bible Church International who accepted me as one of their own. He has personally been a mentor, elder, big brother, encourager, and even father figure. He has spoken things directly into my life that has helped me to grow in the Lord and in life in general.

And Last but not least, to the (4) children that were entrusted to me "spiritually" before biologically having children of my own: **My Cenia, BJ, Jazz,** and **Yaya;** you started my journey into fatherhood. I thank God that he chose you! I thank God that he chose me. I thank you all for allowing me to do so unto this present day to the best of my ability. You all will always hold a special place in my heart.

Corey R. Washington Sr.

Introduction

When I sit and contemplate the present state and condition of our nation and country, I am presented with the question, "If not now, when?" When I sit and consider the many atrocities that we see and face daily in the form of crime and thefts, mass shootings and murders within our communities and neighborhoods, I consider to myself again: "If not now, when?"

When I wake up in a world that has suffered from the devastation of a "pandemic" and virus that has wiped out over 500 million people worldwide (and counting), again I cannot get away from the question, "If not now, when? You see, as a "front line worker" at a hospital in New York City, I have seen some of the most horrific and disturbing things enter the emergency room that blew my mind and crushed my heart but never, and I mean ever have I seen anything like this deadly pandemic that ushered human bodies out of hospitals around the city into refrigerated trucks at an alarming rate; one on top of the other only to be emptied and brought back at designated spots to do it all over again! This lasted for months. Many who were here with us one minute was literally gone the next.

So you might be asking yourself at this point, what is it with him and this question, and what does it have to do with me? Well, "I am glad that you asked!" If not now, when will you make it right with that loved one, that friend, or that family member? If not now, when will you reach out to your children, perhaps that you haven't seen or spoken to in years?

If not now, when will you begin to have the "hard conversations" with those you love and care about, which most definitely will render you vulnerable? If not now, when will you let go of your bitterness and resentment, your anger and hate towards people who may have mistreated you and done you wrong? How long will you allow this to eat away at you like a cancer? How much more of the short time that you have on this earth will you live haphazardly in such a state? If not now, when will you stop blaming your Mother or your Father and your past for your present life? When will you stop blaming "everybody else" for where you are in life today without taking any accountability at all?

If not now, when will you step out in faith regarding all the things you hope and wish to do and be? When will you step out and write that book or start that business? When will you create that brand, start that record label, or make that album? When will you relocate and purchase that dream home, or perhaps change positions/careers when presented that fear has crippled you from doing so?

Well, guess what? I believe that if you have not started to do so already, if you are reading this book, your "when is now!" Tomorrow is not promised, today is not yet over, and yesterday is out of reach. So I ask you, what will you do with your "here and now?"Let me leave you with something to ponder upon while you tackle these "life-changing" questions and decide your next steps:

"Yesterday is not ours to recover, but tomorrow is ours to win or lose." – Lyndon B. Johnson

Whatsoever you put your hands to do, do it with all of your might; because there is no work, nor plan of doing, nor knowledge, or wisdom, in the grave where we are all going at one time or another! Ecclesiastes 9:10 (Emphasis added).

The meaning of life is to find your gift. The purpose of life is to give it away – Pablo Picasso.

So, are you ready! Let's begin to "write our way out" into the places we were created for! It's time to "write your vision" and to make it plain in order that you may run and excel in it accordingly!

Corey R. Washington Sr.

Prelude

God, investigate my life. Get all the facts firsthand. I'm an open book to you. Even from a distance, you know what I'm thinking. You know when I leave and when I get back. I'm never out of your sight. You know everything I'm going to say before I start the first sentence. I look behind me, and you're there, then up ahead and you're there, too - your reassuring presence, coming and going. This is too much, too wonderful - I can't take it all in!

Is there any place I can go to avoid your Spirit and be out of your sight? If I climb to the sky, you're there! If I go underground, you're there! If I flew on morning's wings to the far western horizon, you'd find me in a minute - you're already there waiting! Then I said to myself, "Oh, he even sees me in the dark! At night I'm immersed in the light!"

It's a fact: darkness isn't dark to you; night and day, darkness and light, they're all the same to you. Oh yes, you shaped me first inside, then out; you formed me in my mother's womb. I thank you, High God-you're breathtaking! Body and soul, I am marvelously made! I worship in adoration - what a creation! You know me inside and out. You know every bone in my body; you know exactly how I was made, bit by bit, how I was sculpted from nothing into something. Like an open book, you watched me grow from conception to birth; all the stages of my life were spread out before you. The days of my life were all prepared before I'd even lived one day.

Your thoughts - how rare, how beautiful! God, I'll never comprehend them! I couldn't even begin to count them - any more than I could count the sand of the sea. Oh, let me rise in the morning and live always with you!

Psalms 139:1-18. The Message

Chapter 1
Write The Vision and Make it Plain

If not now, when?
The roadmap for Planning, Proclaiming, and Pursuing your Purpose, with Purpose

Write the vision and make it plain
Have you ever asked yourself such questions as: What is my purpose? What role do I play in the ministry or in life in general? How do I get there? How do I execute such? What career do I choose? What school should I attend? Where should I live? And even if you have chosen a school already, what do I major in? If you have asked yourself such questions, then you have, in Fact, already inquired to some degree about the vision for your life, and you are not alone! We all have asked or will ask such questions over the course of our lives because what we have inside of us will not let us rest until we answer it or die ignoring it. You see, we have the DNA and the greatness of a God on the inside of us waiting to emerge and come forth to show a part of him through us upon the earth. *"Let us make man in our likeness and our image"* is what God says in the very beginning of creation in **Genesis Chapter 1:26."** There-

fore, he displays a part of himself in and through us every time our vision is manifested because the vision in actuality belongs to him. He has put deep down on the inside of us those things that drive us, those things that we are gifted to do with ease and without being paid to do over the course of our lives. For example, if you are a person who loves to minister and serve people, chances are you did not just start being that person. If you are an encourager and motivator with the gift of helping others, then I am quite sure that this was something that you have done most of your life (if not all), even if you were unaware of such. A pastor who is ordained today was not a Pastor at birth (naturally speaking), although he may have been so (spiritually speaking), as one ordained by God to be so. Let me explain.

Write Your Way Out:

In the Book of Jeremiah, the word of God is stated as follows: "Then the word of the Lord came to me, saying, before I formed you in the belly I knew you; and before you were born (or came out of your mother's womb I sanctified you, and Ordained you a Prophet to the nations." Jeremiah 1:4-5. Emphasis added.

As you can clearly see, Jeremiah was a Prophet first spiritually speaking. He was sanctified and ordained by God to be such before he was ever in his mother's womb! This was before ever walking in the office naturally. In addition, naturally speaking, he would have to develop into being a Prophet as he walked with God. So it is with you and me. What we are and the gifts that were given to us was done before we were ever thought about or used any of them!

So when I mention the word vision to you, what comes to mind? *The Merriam Webster's Dictionary defines vision as:* the ability to see; sight or eyesight; something that you imagine; a picture that you see or dream, especially as part of a religious or supernatural experience. So in layman's terms, my vision is something that I can imagine and see. This is important. *Muhammad Ali was quoted as saying, "the man who has no imagination has no wings."* To me, this simply means that we can go no further than our imaginations can take us. As good as Mr. Ali's statement about imagination was, there is no greater statement regarding imagination as far as I am concerned than this: *"Imagination is more important than knowledge. Knowledge is limited. Imagination encircles the world." – Albert Einstein.* This is because it defines what the wings are that Muhammad Ali spoke of earlier and what they were capable of doing. The imagination is the wings that encircle the world. I personally like to think of vision as a brand, idea, strategy, target and success. The word "brand" sticks out to me more than them all. You see, just as Nike, Gucci, Sony, and Mercedes Benz, to name a few are all global businesses, they are also exclusively brands or Ideas that belong solely to the visionaries. For example, there are many McDonald's franchises that are independently owned yet still remain a McDonald's that must adhere to the quality and standards of the brand. Even if they were to sell their companies to someone else, they would forever remain the brand that they were originally created to be, yet still remain a McDonald's and adhere to the quality and standards of that brand. Hence, your vision is always original! It is something that cannot be duplicated or accomplished by anyone else. Your vision is unique because you are unique. You are fearfully and wonderfully made. Psalms 139:14.

Imagination is indispensable to vision

Imagination is imperative to moving in and discovering the vision for our lives. The bible declares: **as a man thinks in his heart, so is he." Prov: 23:7.** This simply means that what we think we are, we do, and we become. In the field of counseling, Cognitive Behavioral Therapy (CBT) suggests that our thoughts create our feelings, and our feelings/emotions create our behavior, and our behavior produces an action or outcome as a result. According to the word of God and therapist, what we think has a great deal to do with who we are, what we do, and who we become. Another reference regarding the power of imagination is recorded in **Genesis Chapter 11:1-9** where the Babylonians decided that they were going to build a city and tower up to heaven. In response to their actions, God looks down and states that because their language was one language, and because they were one people in unity, nothing would be restrained from them, which they have **imagined** to do! Emphasis added. In short, God had to come down and confound their language. He had to stop them from accomplishing what they had **imagined** to do for themselves by building a city and tower to heaven. They were not building something for God.

They were building something that they envisioned would make them equal with Him. The Point: First, your vision must be God's vision for your life, or it will not be permitted. Secondly, Imagination is the wings that Muhammad Ali spoke of and the substance that Albert Einstein stated as, "encircling the world." When we harness the power of imagination that is in line with and centered on the word of God, possibilities are limitless! Simply put, this is thinking and imagining according to all of the great and wonderful things that He has done for us and all of the things that He said we are, could have, could do, and be.

Write the vision and make it plain

Now let us explore where the principle of "writing the vision" comes from. In the book of Habakkuk, starting from the first chapter, the Prophet Habakkuk questions God's judgment regarding what he believes are injustices. He describes to God how he cries, and God does not hear. He says that he even

Write Your Way Out: If Not Now, When?

calls out "violence," and God does not save. In short, the Prophet declares that "the law is powerless." How many times have you felt as such because of the many wrongs and injustices that you may have had to suffer? Habakkuk declares that "justice never comes." **Hab 1:1-4 Emphasis added.** And then God answers Habakkuk in verse 5! The reply of the Lord to the prophet is this: *"Look among the nations and watch- be utterly astounded and amazed! For I will work in your days, while you are still alive (that will counteract your concerns) which you would not believe, though it were told you.* Here is the beginning of the vision for Habakkuk, and here begins the visions of you and me. I am sent to tell you that today is the day, and these are the days and times!

Again, the Lord answers the Prophet in chapter 2 after Habakkuk complains yet again, still in Chapter 1:13-17. **(Read chapters 1 and 2).** The Lord now responds in chapter 2 after the Prophet starts off by saying the following words, which are crucial to understanding the origin, principle, and power of writing out a vision:*"I will stand guard and watch and place myself on the rampart, which* is defined as follows: *A defensive wall of a castle or walled city, having a broad top and walkway and typically a stone parapet.* This is a place that is high up with a broad top. I immediately envision standing atop a mountain and looking out across a broad spectrum of sights far and wide as the eye could see, which makes all the sense in the world to me because a true vision is always far beyond what a human mind and heart can envision or receive.

This is because the vision is God in you, the hope of glory! The Prophet says that from here he will watch, even from a broad place, because to see your vision, you must see it as God sees it! You must see it through the eyes of God. It takes a "broad place" mindset to see and comprehend such. But then, the Prophet says that "he will watch."

Watch what? *I will watch to see what he will say to me!* Get the understanding. He will watch and wait to see the physical manifestations of what God *speaks* to him! So do we write our visions! We must be able to see them in order to write them. Every word that God speaks to us is substance! Just as he spoke and created something out of nothing by the power and substance of his word, so is every word that he speaks to us. This is why we are to speak whatever we have need of and create it because, in all actuality, the word is alive, active, powerful, and sharper than a two-edged sword! Heb **4:12**.

The word is *spirit* and *life*, so it has its own creative ability and power within it. The bible declares that *"the words that he speaks to us are both spirit and life."* So we must use our voice to speak our visions into existence just as our God and father did when he created the world. We were made in his likeness and image! We are able to create only because we use our voice to speak his words; however, *"the angels hearken to the voice of his word." Psalm 103:20.* They are not listening and paying attention to my words; they are doing so according to his words that I lend my voice to! His word has its own voice. Likewise, angels are "Ministering" spirits sent to serve those who will inherit salvation? *Hebrews 1:14. In other words, angels are sent to assist those who will become fellow members and believers of the body of Christ as well as those who already are.* Remember, it is only God who knows your life from before the beginning until its end!

So, as the Lord answered Habakkuk, he answers you and me today: "Write your vision and make it plain upon tablets, so that he may run who reads it! It is not yet time for the vision to come true, but that time is coming soon; the vision will come true. It may seem like a long time, but be patient and wait for it because it will surely come to pass, and it will not be delayed." **Hab 2:2-3. Emphasis added**.

Somebody is waiting for you to write your vision. Somebody's life depends upon it! And then God is so good that he allows you and your family to reap the benefits of doing so! A true vision will always be bigger than yourself and bless a

Write Your Way Out: If Not Now, When?

multitude of people, which in turn blesses you for being obedient. This is the difference between a "God vision and a good vision." You see, when God determined that Christ would die for us, he envisioned the outcome of mankind being restored to him in fellowship, worship, and relationship. His vision and purpose for doing so was for the whole world! Likewise, the vision that is written and made plain and has running in it for the carrier and the reader must be written with the same mindset. I decree, declare and prophesy that if you are reading this book, you will run with your vision in the name of Jesus Christ that will bless a multitude of peoples, tongues, kindreds and nations!

Chapter 2
Write Your Way Out

The roadmap that connects you to your Divine assignment and place of being.

Notice that I said, *"Your divine assignment"* as it pertains to your giftings and callings followed by *"your place of being."* This is more than or in addition to your divine assignment and calling as it pertains to the ministry or your profession etc. This is the very existence and being that is birthed from your divine assignment. This place of being will always derive from and be a byproduct of the characteristics and calling upon your life. In addition, your place of being will always take you outside of the place that you are at presently. It extends farther than your church or ministry. It reaches farther than your job or profession. The bible declares that *"gifts and callings are without repentance." Romans 11:29.* Or in other words, the gifts, talents, and abilities that are given to us before birth are *"irrevocable."* We all have been given gifts and talents and abilities. These gifts are not predicated upon whether or not "you are spiritual" or attend a church. We all have something unique to do and contribute to this world, no matter how big or small. These gifts and callings cannot be taken back. They are ours whether we use them or not. They remain ours whether we ever realize that we have been gifted with certain abilities and talents or not. They are ours whether we ever attribute such from coming from and being granted by God himself or not. It has often been said that the grave is one of the richest places on earth because so many people have died with all of the gifts, talents, and abilities that God gave them buried inside, both figuratively and literally. God forbid that this would be our portion!

In lieu of this, I am reminded of being at the Potter's House in Dallas, Texas where I had the opportunity and privilege to see the Bishop T.D. Jakes in person for the first time who preached like never before. If you have ever seen him on T.V. or heard him on a CD and think that you have really experienced him, you have not! For as many years as I saw him in this manner, I was always blessed beyond measure. However, it was not until I witnessed him preach in person that I came to understand that there was more to his precision and delivery as if it could be more to him, I asked myself! I can only imagine after experiencing what I did for just one service what the Potters House and those who are closest to him experience on a daily basis. I have personally watched him and followed him for years. I am in no way affiliated with him personally, neither am I using this *"reference"* and nugget of wisdom and knowledge as an endorsement or anything else for that matter. I am solely doing so in order to *"make plain"* what I am expressing. The Sunday morning that I was in attendance, he preached a message entitled, *"Grasping the moment."* I highly recommend that you watch it if you have not done so already. This particular message was centered on "Jacob and Esau" and how Jacob tricked Esau out of his birthright. In short, grasping the moment was really about seizing the many opportunities that present themselves to us in the moment, as in, "the time is now."

The roadmap that connects you to your Divine assignment and place of being.

On another occasion, I heard him say that "he is more than

a preacher" and will not be defined only as such. For many religious people, this could be considered blasphemy! However, when you take into account that he is a businessman, a bestselling author, a movie writer, actor and producer, a T.V. host, a leader to leaders and pastors, and a spiritual advisor to Gov't officials, (and I am quite sure that I have left something out), it would appear to me that this confirms that he is more than just a pastor! He is far more than what society and we as a people have deemed him to be. I was almost inclined to use the word *"doomed"* him to be instead of deemed because, in actuality, if we don't know who we are, we will become or stay the person that we are right now instead of evolving into our places of being! In all actuality, pastoring, preaching and teaching is how many of us know him, including myself. Again, I am not personally connected to him. However, it appears to me that one of the keys to him becoming who he is, has been tied to him not allowing society or people to define and limit him to just being one thing.

Write Your Way Out

What we allow to define us becomes our reality and our limitation. The subtlety of it all is that there is nothing wrong with being a pastor, or in ministry, or a professional, etc. It is only when we allow what we are defined by (whether positive and especially negative) to keep us in one place instead of constantly evolving that we are robbed of entering into **"our places of being"** and promised lands. One would only think that you would have to watch out for those things and people who define you in negative ways! Not so!

In fact, I am inclined to believe that I am not, nor can I even be in the will of God as a **"one-time event,"** or just because I might be at the moment if I am not in **"my place of being"** because, there are some things that he will tell me to do, or not to do for that matter, that will continue to determine if I am in his will or not hence; we must always move and evolve in him. The bible declares in *Exodus Chapter 13:20-21 that "the lord went before them in a pillar of cloud by day, and a pillar of fire by night to give them light to lead them."* Emphasis added. Again, in **Numbers chapter 9:17-23**, the bible is clear regarding the leading and the following of God, and Holy Spirit:

"when the cloud moved from its place over the tent, the Israelites moved, and wherever the cloud stopped, the Israelites camped. So the Israelites moved at the Lord's command, and they camped at his command. While the cloud stayed over the tent, they remained camped. Sometimes the cloud stayed over the tent for a long time, but the Israelites obeyed the Lord and did not move. Sometimes the cloud was over for only a few days. At the Lord's command, the people camped, and at his command, they moved.

Sometimes the cloud stayed only from dusk till dawn. When the cloud lifted the next morning, the people moved. When the cloud lifted day or night, the people moved. The cloud might stay over the tent for two days, a month, or a year. As long as it stayed, the people camped, but when it lifted, they moved. At the Lord's command, the people camped, and at his command they moved. They obeyed the Lord's order that he commanded through Moses. NCV.

Write Your Way Out

According to this detailed account of obedience and leading of God and the Holy Spirit, could there be many of us who are in ministry and on jobs and even in relationships that are not in *"their places of being"* because they are stagnant? That place of ministry or the job, or your relationship, could very well be a divine place, as was the tent and its location, but not your place of being, because in your place of being, you are constantly moving and evolving. In your place of *being,* you never become, in the sense of becoming all that you are, you are forever "being" molded and shaped into your divine place of being. Your place of being is that place that transcends outside of the four walls of the church and the ministry or your job and profession, although divinely speaking, it is the place and genesis of its existence and origin. That place of being will allow you and your mate to flow from your own autonomies while still remaining one. How do I know this? Because each one of us are fearfully and wonderfully made! Your vision will also always take you past the four walls of the church and where you currently are because imagination has wings that encircle the world. The world is far beyond your church and your job.

For instance, according to the scriptures, Jesus Christ always existed; even before the foundation of the world; however, he did not come into his place of being until he was born of a Virgin, reared as a child into an adult, and then prepared for the calling and assignment for his life although divinely existent. So his divinity is not in question here, and I suppose neither is your divine assignment. It is our place of being that we have to wait on and work at.

Again, the Prophet Jeremiah was chosen and ordained and appointed as such before he was ever thought about being conceived by earthly methods, however, his place of being was not. This was something that he too, had to wait for, work at, and be prepared for. Your place of being is more than your divine assignment; it is walking out the perfect will of God for your life in more areas than just the church. It transcends past the four walls into the world, although it is always centered in and flows from your divine assignment, callings and giftings. In your place of being, you are no longer doing or being something or someone. ***You just simply are!***

Write Your Way Out

So now what?

So logically speaking, the first thing that we have to do in order to begin to "write our way out" of mediocrity into our places of being is to be "transformed by the renewing of our minds." **Romans 12:1-2 is recorded as saying; "be not conformed or fashioned or live according to this world and its desires, rather be transformed or changed and made new by the renewing of your mind." Emphasis added.** This is a daily process and decision to allow our minds to be changed from a way of thinking that, in actuality, is self-defeating. This way of thinking has been inherited by our fallen natures in addition to our upbringings, cultures, backgrounds and world views.

Secondly, we must use the weapons that God has granted us to pull down such mindsets and self-defeating thinking that oppose and speak against God's very best for us. Corinthians chapter 10:3-5 states, *"although we are human beings, we are not fighting against human beings or by human methods, the weapons we use to fight with are not earthly such as knives and guns, but they are spiritual and mighty through God to the pulling down of strongholds, casting down imaginations and every high thing that exalts itself higher than the knowledge of God and what he said that we could do, be, and have. And by doing so, we make every one of those evil, self- defeating thoughts obey Christ and his word over our lives for us. Emphasis added.* As long as I have known this scripture and even preached and taught from it, it did not really come to life for me until I heard a great man and teacher say; *"Listen to what your inner voice is saying to you."* Only then can I begin to confront, block, and cast down such negative thoughts and thinking and replace them with positive ones.

A *stronghold* as defined is: a place that has been fortified or strengthened so as to protect it from attack." Something that has been fortified in this manner allows nothing to get in or nothing to get out. In addition, a stronghold is a place where a particular cause or belief is strongly defended or upheld. So a stronghold over my mind and thinking could look like this: I will never be anything. I will live like this all my life. I will always live in poverty, lack, want, and defeat. Nobody loves me or cares for me. Even, it would be better for me to end my life than continue to live this way! Simply put, a stronghold is a fixed and deeply rooted way of thinking that has become fortified and has a "strong-hold" over the way we look at life and at people. Once such thoughts are rehearsed over and over through the course of our lives, they become a "fortified stronghold and fortress." Next, as the text suggests, they are **imaginations** that are self-defeating.

Write Your Way Out

Also notice that an *"imagination"* speaks to that of the mind and our thoughts. One way or the other, in actuality, we will write out our visions for our lives that will manifest for *"better or for worse."* Could this be the reason why so many of us are where we are at in life because we have written our visions already? I strongly believe so! I say this because I also believe that God created us to imagine and to harness the power of our minds and imaginations to create just as he did. We were made in his likeness and image. I also can tell you that this was the reason why he came down to confound the language of the Babylonians, as stated earlier, because of the potential and the power of imagination. If you are like me, then you know that it is time for us to "rewrite the visions for our lives to conform to what God says that we can do, be, and have. Mahatma Gandhi said it like this: *"A man is but the product of his thoughts. What he thinks, he becomes!* "Never say anything about yourself that you don't want to come true"- **anonymous**. The word of God instructs us to: "Let this mind be in you, which was also in Christ Jesus." Philippians 2:5-11. Next, write out your vision on a vision board, poster or wall (where applicable) so that you can visualize what it is that you are reaching for. Habakkuk chapter 2:2 states *"write the vision and make it plain upon tablets, so that he may run who reads it."* Notice that the scripture says, "So he may run who reads it." In actuality, the one who reads will run as well as the one who writes! That's why it is so important to "write it out" so that you can see it and then speak it. According to Psalm chapter 45:1, we are also to speak what is written in our visions. *"My thoughts are filled with beautiful words for the king, and I will use my voice as a writer would use pen and ink. CEV.* This is not just speaking; this is speaking prophetically! We are to use our voices as a writer would use pen and ink, thus painting the canvases of our visions into existence.

Next, surrounding yourself with individuals who speak to the greatness that is within you while also challenging and stretching you to be the very best you is crucial. *"Where no counsel is, the people fail; but in the multitude of counselors there is safety. Proverbs 11:14.* Also, *"faith comes by hearing, and hearing by the word of God" Romans 10:17.* Coincidently, fear *(false evidence appearing real)* comes by hearing as well. Who you surround yourself with will determine the level and altitude that you reach. Who you surround yourself with will determine your progress or your procrastination. I cannot stress this point enough! There was something that I recently saw on social media that I want to share with you that blessed me tremendously. After reading it, I was astounded. I guess because I never personally looked at it this way. "A shark in a fish tank will grow 8 inches, but in the ocean, it will grow up to 8 feet or more! The shark will never outgrow its environment and the same is true about you. Many times we're around small-thinking people, so we don't grow.

Change your environment and watch your growth. What's amazing to me is that this is the same shark! Not a different species but the same one! Both sharks have within them the same DNA and abilities and attributes; however, it is only when the shark's territory was enlarged that he grew into his unlimited potential and size; even its true place of being! In fact, the shark would have never known the true potential that he possessed! As a dear friend and colleague of mine described it, "we can remain the biggest fish in the pond and remain the same or allow ourselves to be the smallest amongst those who are great." In doing so, we actually tap into all of the resources and space that they occupy!

Lastly, rely on the person and presence of the Holy Spirit to teach, direct, guide and lead you into all the truth of your vision and life and all truth in general. *The bible declares in Psalms 91:1, "Live under the protection of God most high and stay in and under the shadow of God All-Powerful." CEV.* This is the place where we are covered and sheltered to hear and receive the downloads and revelations of God via the Holy Spirit concerning our lives and visions etc.

In the secret place, the principalities and powers and spiritual wickedness and rulers in high places cannot stop, deflect, nor re-route such revelation because they are not allowed nor permitted here. This is why the Holy Spirit is with us in the earth; to Glorify Jesus and to make known to us what the son reveals to Him. John 16:14

Listen what the sovereign Lord declares: *Do not forget this! Keep it in mind! Remember this, you guilty ones. Remember the things I have done in the past. For I alone am God! I am God, and there is none like me. Only I can tell you the future before it happens. Everything I plan will come to pass, for I do whatever I wish. Isaiah 46:8-10 New Living Translation.*

Before you move on to the next chapters, implement the following steps to begin creating and writing your vision and making it plain!

Chapter 3
The Writing Is On The Wall

Can you see it?

One night as I was about to lay down to go to bed around 11:30-12 midnight, I had just hung up the phone as I was having a conversation with a spiritual friend and colleague. I really needed and wanted to just crash at this point. I turned my light out, turned my T.V. off, and as soon as my head hit the pillow, literally, I heard, *"The writing is on the wall."* I knew immediately that it was the Lord speaking to me. I knew he was trying to convey something to me. At first, I equated the "writing is on the wall" with the Vision boards that I have posted up on my walls but felt as though it was something more that the Lord was trying to say to me. I then responded, **"Lord, what is it"? I am tired, Lord. I want to go to sleep, literally. I am often awakened or kept up late at night hearing and writing, which is how the majority of this book was written.** I then said to myself, I will research this thing in the morning but realized that I would probably not even remember this in the morning. And even if I did, some pertinent information and revelation would be lost because it is only when we move instantly that we are benefited from what He has for us in a thing.

I got up and grabbed my phone (It's a millennial thing), and went to the book of Daniel Chapter 5, where we will begin to lay the foundation. Belshazzar, the king, was the son of Nebuchadnezzar, who used the vessels of the temple of God and worshipped other gods. He used the Holy things of God with concubines and his princes and worshipped and served other gods. Beginning at verse 4, the bible states: as they drank the wine, they praised the gods of gold and silver, of bronze, iron, wood and stone. In short, today's definition of a concubine would be a "mistress" or a "side chick." With this in mind, one could only imagine what else was taking place in such an environment.

Suddenly the fingers of a human hand appeared and wrote on the plaster of the wall, near the lampstand in the royal palace. *The king watched the hand as it wrote.* His face turned pale, and he was so frightened that his knees knocked together, and his legs gave way. Could you imagine seeing a hand and fingers without a body attached writing on your walls?

I am reminded of the time when Jesus responded to the Scribes and Pharisees who accused him of casting out Devils (evil spirits) by the power of Beelzebub (devil) saying, *"But if I with the finger of God cast out devils make no mistakes about it that the kingdom of God is come upon you!" Luke 11:20 & Matthew 12:28.* The kingdom of God came to deal with the king and his pride! As the story goes, the king becomes terrified to the point of his loins being smote with weakness. Loins in biblical times always referred to a man's strength, vigor, and stamina. The king then calls out for his hired enchanters, astrologers and diviners (witches, warlocks, and wizards) to be brought in and said to these wise men of Babylon, "Whoever reads this writing and tells me what it means will be clothed in purple and have a gold chain placed around his neck, and he will be made the third highest ruler in the kingdom." The color purple in biblical times was synonymous with "royalty, stature, and position," while gold was a symbol of wealth.

Write Your Way Out: If Not Now, When?

Then all the king's wise men came in, but they could not read the writing or tell the king what it meant. So King Belshazzar became even more terrified, and his face grew paler. His nobles were baffled. I am here to tell you that the enemy could not read the interpretation thereof then, neither can he read it now when you write saith the spirit of Grace! All of the hosts of hell cannot read nor interpret what is written because there are some things that have yet to be written by you and me. *The word of the Lord declares, "If every one of them were written down, I suppose that even the whole world would not have room or be able to contain the books that would be written! John 21:25 Emphasis added. There are some things that Jesus has done for us that are not even known to man nor angels! They already exist. We just have to write them into existence as he releases the vision to us. Daniel was recorded as saying, "I, Daniel, was the only one who saw the vision; those who were with me did not see it, but such terror overwhelmed them that they fled and hid themselves. So I was left alone, gazing at this great vision; I had no strength left, my face turned deathly pale and I was helpless. Then I heard him speaking, and as I listened to him, I fell into a deep sleep, with my face to the ground.* Believe it or not, contrary to what Christendom may tell you, there are some things that are only reserved and revealed to you individually as a visionary! Then those who are connected with you will catch on in the spirit and align themselves with you to assist you in carrying it out.

The queen, hearing the voices of the king and his nobles, came into the banquet hall. "O king, live forever!" she said. "Don't be alarmed! Don't look so pale! There is a man in your kingdom that has the spirit of the holy gods in him. In the time of your father, he was found to have insight and intelligence and wisdom like that of the gods. **King Nebuchadnezzar your father--your father the king, I say--appointed him chief of the magicians, enchanters, astrologers and diviners.** This man Daniel, whom the king called Belteshazzar, was found to have a keen mind and knowledge and understanding, and also the ability to interpret dreams, explain riddles, and solve difficult problems. **Call for Daniel, and he will tell you what the writing means."** So Daniel was brought before the king, and the king said to him, "Are you Daniel, one of the exiles my father the king brought from Judah? Notice that Daniel was referred to as an *"exile." Or in other words, one who is barred or evicted for punitive reasons.* Daniel was placed in the lion's den because he would not bow down and worship the king hence: being in exile is always the atmosphere and environment to hear and receive the prophetic!

It is a place that is designated for such encounters with God. The Apostle John was on the Island of Patmos in prison for the word of God and his testimony, where he heard unspeakable mysteries and revelations from God. Rev 1:9-11. Thus today, we have the "Book of Revelation." What have you been "barred or evicted from" because you don't fit into the status quo bubble? What have you been evicted and barred from because of the vision that is within you that contradicts what you are presently seeing and experiencing? The king goes on to say, I have heard that the spirit of the gods is in you and that you have insight, intelligence and outstanding wisdom. **The wise men and enchanters were brought before me to read this writing and to tell me what it means, but they could not explain it.** Now I have heard that you are able to give interpretations and to solve difficult problems. If you can read this writing and tell me what it means, you will be clothed in purple and have a gold chain placed around your neck, and you will be made the third highest ruler in the kingdom."

Then Daniel answered the king, "You may keep your gifts for yourself and give your rewards to someone else. Nevertheless, I will read the writing for the king and tell him what it means. Then, Daniel begins to interpret the writing for the king:

"O king, the Most High God gave your father Nebuchadnezzar sovereignty and greatness and glory and splendor. Because of the high position he gave him, all the peoples and nations and men of every language dreaded and feared him. Those the king wanted to put to death, he put to death; those he wanted to spare, he spared; those he wanted to promote, he promoted; and those he wanted to humble, he humbled. But when his heart became arrogant and hardened with pride, he was deposed from his royal throne and stripped of his glory. He was driven away from people and given the mind of an animal; he lived with the wild donkeys and ate grass like cattle; and his body was drenched with the dew of heaven until he acknowledged that the Most High God is sovereign over the kingdoms of men and sets over them anyone he wishes. It got so bad for the king because of his pride that the bible says that he was "driven away from the sons of men; his heart was made like that of a beast; and he became one who ate grass like animals. All this because he did not humble himself before God.

Then to make matters worse, because his son Belshazzar knew all of this and did not humble himself and his heart before God, the hand of God and the writing was sent to him as judgment as well. Isn't it funny how a generation can either perpetuate the sins of their fathers or stop it in its tracks?

The word goes on to say: "But you, his son, O Belshazzar, have not humbled yourself, though you knew all this. Instead, you have set yourself up against the Lord of heaven. You had the goblets from his temple brought to you, and you and your nobles, your wives and your concubines drank wine from them. You praised the gods of silver and gold, of bronze, iron, wood and stone, which cannot see or hear or understand.

But you did not honor the God who holds in his hand your life and all your ways. Therefore he sent the hand that wrote the inscription."

This Is The Inscription That Was Written:

MENE, MENE, TEKEL, PARSINE

This Is What These Words Mean:

Mene: God has numbered the days of your reign and brought it to an end.

Tekel: You have been weighed on the scales and found wanting.

Amplified Bible: You have been weighed on the scales of (Righteousness) and found deficient. The bible declares that "in righteousness God judges and makes war. Rev: 19:11.

Peres: Your kingdom is divided and given to the Medes and Persians."

Then at Belshazzar's command, Daniel was clothed in purple, a gold chain was placed around his neck, and he was proclaimed the third highest ruler in the kingdom. The writing on the wall is said to mean that there are clear signs that something will fail or no longer exist. According to the third chapter of Daniel, the writing that appeared on the wall to the king was for just that reason. And this is why I believe that he allowed me to hear these words on this night: to let me know that every spirit of pride and every spirit that has exalted itself over my life would "fail or no longer exist." So does he write to you today In the name of Jesus Christ! I decree and declare and prophesy that the Lord has written to every one of your enemies with the "hand of a man" that has truly come to steal, to kill, and to destroy you; those who overpowered you and exploited you to their own benefits and literally acted as if they were God over you the following to our adversaries, (and I am not referring to people) because we do not wage war against flesh and blood (People) rather principalities and powers and spiritual wickedness and rulers in high places (Eph 6:10-12):

. . .

Write Your Way Out: If Not Now, When?

Mene: God has numbered the days of your reign and brought it to an end. Tekel: You have been weighed on the scales and found wanting.

Peres: Your kingdom is divided and given to the Medes and Persians.

"When you write your vision saith the Spirit of grace, you are the "hand of a man doing the writing!"

That very night Belshazzar, king of the Babylonians, was slain, and Darius the Mede took over the kingdom at the age of sixty-two. This very night so is the writing on the wall interpreted for you! Now decree and declare and prophesy what is written against the Spirit of pride in and over your life by the hands of those who ruled and exalted themselves over you and prevented and delayed the Lord's vision through you to come to pass in the name of Jesus Christ!

Chapter 4
The Significance Of the Hand and Writing

The Significance of the Hand and Writing

Handwriting is an essential skill for both children and adults. For younger children, handwriting is said to activate the brain more than keyboarding because it involves more complex motor and cognitive skills. Handwriting is also said to contribute to reading fluency because it activates the visual perception of letters. Writing goes as far back as the writing of the Ten Commandments on two stone tablets by God himself! In today's society, there are several different types of writing skills most commonly used, and they are as follows: *Expository, Descriptive, Narrative, Persuasive and Creative writing.*

1. *Expository writing* is *writing* that seeks to explain, illuminate or 'expose' (which is where the word *'expository'* comes from).
2. *Descriptive writing* is used to describe a person, place or thing in such a way that a picture is formed in the reader's mind. Capturing an event through *descriptive writing* involves paying close attention to the details by using all of your five senses.

3. *Narrative writing* is *writing* that has a story, characters, conflict, and other essential parts of a story. *Narrative writing* is often synonymous with a story. And this differs greatly compared to other forms of *writing,* like in textbooks and certain nonfiction books.
4. *Persuasive writing* is a form of nonfiction *writing* that encourages careful word choice, the development of logical arguments, and a cohesive summary.
5. *Creative writing* is a form of *writing* where *creativity* is at the forefront of its purpose through using imagination, *creativity,* and innovation in order to tell a story through strong written visuals with an emotional impact, like in poetry *writing,* short story *writing,* novel *writing,* and more.

It is important to know and understand that these forms of writing skills began before the foundation of the world with our God! As he spoke things into existence, he was, in actuality, writing what would be. The word of God is written with each of these writing skills in mind because the Bible declares that *"the words that he speaks to us are both spirit and life."* This means that his word is not like an ordinary book that we read. It is much more than that. When we read his words, we are supposed to be able to tap into the picture and presence of what it is that he is saying and conveying through his word. We are supposed to be able to see the picture that he is painting of his word which is the canvas. This is because he is the word made flesh! So his desire is to manifest himself to us in any of the above-mentioned formats through his word. This, of course, in spirit. If you consider any of the above-mentioned writing skills, they all have an element of the use of "imagination" and cognitive abilities.

So does the word of God, which cannot be deciphered

merely by intellect. Deep calls unto deep, so does the spirit and life of his word to our spirits and eternal life within. The hand is the most frequently symbolized part of the human body. It gives blessings, and it is expressive. According to Aristotle, the hand is the *"tool of tools."* In general it is strength, power and protection. However, it can just as easily mean generosity, hospitality and stability. (Umich.edu.)

The usage of the word *"hand"* in the Hebrew *(yadh)* is associated with strength, authority, and power. Thus the term "hand" is associated with *power in the hand."* This is why Jesus is stated as being "seated at the right hand of the father," even at the place of power and authority and strength and honor! See Ephesians 1:20 and Colossians 3:1.

Again, the word of the Lord records an account when Jesus Christ was "casting out" evil spirits from individuals, and there were some present who stated that he did so by and through the power of Beelzebub, or in other words, (by Satan). Jesus quickly informed them of two things that were important for them to understand. Firstly, a kingdom or city or house divided against itself cannot stand, just as light and darkness cannot coexist at the same time. When you walk into your room, the light is either "on or off." And for those of you who keep a night light on, whichever light is greatest is the governing factor. Next, He highlighted the fact that if He did indeed cast out evil spirits by the power of the one who was the epitome of evil, that he would in fact be divided against Himself. And if so, how would He be able to stand? How would that be advancement for Him and the kingdom He served?

A team that is playing basketball or football does not compete against themselves, neither do they shoot baskets and throw touchdowns on behalf of their opponents. A boxer does not get into the ring and hit himself! It is his intentions and desire to knock his opponent out because they are not on the same team but rather in competition. Likewise, the word states on two separate occasions, once in Luke 11:21 and Mark 3:23 the following:

"When a strong man, fully armed, guards his own house, his possessions are safe. But when someone stronger attacks and overpowers him, he takes away the armor in which the man trusts and divides up his plunder. Lk 11:21

Again, Jesus called them over to Him and began to speak to them in parables:

"How can Satan drive out Satan? If a kingdom is divided against itself, that kingdom cannot stand. If a house is divided against itself, that house cannot stand. And if Satan opposes himself and is divided, he cannot stand; his end has come. In Fact, no one can enter a strong man's house without first tying him up. Then he can plunder the strong man's house. Truly I tell you, people can be forgiven all their sins and every slander they utter, but whoever blasphemes against the Holy Spirit will never be forgiven; they are guilty of an eternal sin." He said this because they were saying, "He has an impure spirit." Mark 3:23. This reminds me of a physical house and dwelling. If the house is divided against itself and its members alike, the house cannot, nor will it stand! James says it like this, "For where envying and strife is, there is confusion and every evil work." James 3:16. So what he was telling them was that "He is not the author of confusion."

But then Jesus tells them, "If I cast out Demons by the finger of God, then surely know that the kingdom of God has come to you! Psalms 144:1 states, blessed be the Lord my strength which teaches my *"hands to war"* and my *"fingers to fight"* glory be to God! Fingers and hands are connected my friends! And every time we write out our visions, we declare war with our hands on everything that opposes us, and then we fight the war with our fingers while writing until we see the manifestation of the written vision! So the word of the Lord to you today is, "write out that vision. " Draw up that business plan! Write out those goals and plans! Write your vision and make it plain! And while you are writing such, this is my prayer for you:

Lord send thine "hand" (Power) from above, rid me, and deliver me out of great waters, even from the "hand" (Power) of strange children, (from those who serve other Gods). Even from those who you are strange to Lord because of the Gods that they have set up to serve in your place in Jesus's name! Psalm 144:7-8. Which "Hand" (Power) are you writing with?

Chapter 5
The Writing Cannot Be Interpreted

The Writing cannot be deciphered or interpreted

As I pondered this reality as recorded in the word of God, I asked myself, 'How could this be?" In spite of reading this, I still struggled to some degree with this statement. Now I understand why. I was looking at such from a humanistic standpoint! I said to myself, if I were to give you something to read, like this book, you would read it and be able to interpret it, especially if you were able to read. So again, that wiped out for me the fact of my "writing" being a thing that could not be deciphered and interpreted until I realized this: the reason why my writing would not be able to be deciphered and interpreted by the enemy or anyone else for that matter is because like Daniel, "I am an original! And so is the vision that God has placed down in me." Listen to what Daniel says again in Chapter 10, verse 7. I, Daniel, was the only one who saw the vision; those who were with me did not see it, but such terror overwhelmed them that they fled and hid themselves. Glory be to God! The enemy cannot read something, nor does he know something that has never been recorded or done before (by man). Hence, my point regarding God only speaking to you individually as it pertains to your vision, no matter the number of people that may be in close proximity to you. It is only those that are connected to your vision that will align themselves to you and assist you in implementing such.

Now, listen to what John says: Now there are also many other things that Jesus did, Were every one of them to be written, I suppose that the world itself could not contain the books that would be written. John 21:25. ESV. Clearly, there are some things that still remain to be seen! Again, another passage of scripture reads as follows: He has put all things in subjection under His feet. For in that He put all things in subjection under Him, He left nothing that is not put under Him. But now, we do not yet see all things put under Him. But we do, however, see Jesus! Hebrews 2:8-9. Glory be to God! All things are under His feet, even the things that are not yet seen! Although they are not yet seen, does not mean that "they are not under His feet," and that we cannot "write them" into being! This simply means that the things that you may not believe are possible or attainable for you because they have never been done, or maybe because others feel so about you, does not mean that this is the case! As a man thinks in his heart, so is he!

Now let's look at the account of Daniel in Chapter 5: Suddenly the fingers of a human hand appeared and wrote on the plaster of the wall, near the lamp-stand in the royal palace. The king watched the hand as it wrote. His face turned pale, and he was so frightened that his legs became weak, and his knees were knocking. (Please note the fingers were of a human hand that wrote)!

The king summoned the enchanters, astrologers and diviners. Then he said to these wise men of Babylon, "Whoever reads this writing and tells me what it means will be clothed in purple and have a gold chain placed around his neck, and he will be made the third highest ruler in the kingdom."

I decree, declare, and prophesy that promotion comes to him who reads and interprets the writings of his God-given vision in the name of Jesus Christ!

Write Your Way Out: If Not Now, When?

The king, in desperation, calls for his hired servants (the powers of darkness) to read and interpret the writing on the wall, but they could not! Then all the king's wise men came in, but they could not read the writing or tell the king what it meant. So King Belshazzar became even more terrified, and his face grew paler. His nobles were baffled.

Notice that the king became "even more terrified" as his face grew pale only when the writing could not be read by his people! I decree, declare, and prophesy that every high place and every altar, every king and Pharaoh and every exalted power over your life will likewise become terrified and pale in the name of Jesus Christ. I decree, declare, and prophesy that they shall no longer know the insights and the inside agendas and messages of your God to you hence, now and forevermore.

The queen, hearing the voices of the king and his nobles, came into the banquet hall. "May the king live forever!" she said. "Don't be alarmed! Don't look so pale! There is a man in your kingdom that has the spirit of the holy gods in him. In the time of your father, he was found to have insight and intelligence, and wisdom like that of the gods. Your father, King Nebuchadnezzar, appointed him chief of the magicians, enchanters, astrologers and diviners. He did this because Daniel, whom the king called Belteshazzar, was found to have a keen mind and knowledge and understanding, and also the ability to interpret dreams, explain riddles and solve difficult problems. Call for Daniel, and he will tell you what the writing means."

I decree, declare, and prophesy to you, Prophet; rise up in the name of Jesus Christ because it has been given to you to interpret and Decipher dreams! It has been granted to you to solve riddles and to solve difficult problems! For such a time as this, were you created and conceived. Now shall you come to the forefront and be thrust into your divine assignment and place of being, even now saith the spirit of grace! So Daniel was brought before the king, and the king said to him, "Are you Daniel, one of the exiles my father, the king, brought from Judah?

I have heard that the spirit of the gods is in you and that you have insight, intelligence and outstanding wisdom. The wise men and enchanters were brought before me to read this writing and tell me what it means, but they could not explain it. Now I have heard that you are able to give interpretations and to solve difficult problems. If you can read this writing and tell me what it means, you will be clothed in purple and have a gold chain placed around your neck, and you will be made the third highest ruler in the kingdom."In the name of Jesus Christ, I decree, declare, and prophesy that the place of exile and prison and slavery that you have been in has been designed to be the place where my divine revelation, wisdom, and understanding could flow to you and reach you. It is only here that you are able to receive the divine impartation's and revelations that can only be transferred to you in such a climate and atmosphere to carry you into your vision and beyond in times of normality saith the spirit of grace. For the wisdom and understanding and the insight that I have given you to interpret such dreams and riddles could only be given in places of exile saith the spirit of grace. You are able to do so because it is I on the inside of you. You need not fear the astrologers nor the enchanters nor the diviners, nor witches, warlocks or wizards because it is I myself who girds and under-girds you saith the Lord thy God! This is your season of promotion within my kingdom and on the earth saith the spirit of grace. Your place of exile was just an incubator where I could hold you long enough to download what you would not have sought me for on your own. Arise my son, arise my daughter, and come up hither saith your Lord and God and get in on the conversation that we are having of you saith the spirit of grace!

After this I looked and saw a door standing open in heaven. And the voice I had previously heard speak to me like a trumpet was saying, "Come up here, and I will show you what must happen after these things."

At once I was in the Spirit, and I saw a throne standing in heaven, with someone seated on it. The One seated there looked like a jasper and carnelian, and a rainbow that gleamed like an emerald encircled the throne. Surrounding the throne was twenty-four other thrones, and on these thrones sat twenty-four elders dressed in white, with golden crowns on their heads. Revelation Chapter 4:1-3. **The writing of your vision cannot be deciphered or interpreted by destiny killers!**

Chapter 6
What is Written Must Come to Pass

What Is Written Must Come To Pass

Have you ever pondered that the word of God is "settled in the heavens?" **Psalms 119:89**. In reality, what does this mean? "Your word, O Lord, lasts forever; it is settled, fixed, and eternal in heaven. **(GNT)**. The word of God declares in the first book of Genesis that God spoke what was in His mind and heart when He said, "Let there be." As a result, what He imagined and then visualized, and what was on His mind, he spoke into existence! I believe that the moment He thought about it, it was already done! In fact, I believe that it was done long before He ever thought or said anything at all because **"He is the word."** In the beginning, the word already existed; the word was **with God**, and the **word was** God. So From the very beginning the word was with God. Through him, God made all things; not one thing in all creation was made without Him. **John Chapter 1:1-3. (GNT)**. The world was created before He ever spoke a word. The speaking of the word was just "spirit and life," manifesting and creating what was already within Him. As a man thinks, in his heart so is he.

As a seed bears fruit after its own kind, we too bear fruit after the *"likeness and image of God!"* Look at Daniels' account of this: In Daniel Chapter 10, the angel of the Lord that appeared to him who was described as being *"sent to him"* was only sent and summoned after the following as recorded: "Since the first day that you set your heart/mind, (which is interchangeable in scripture), to gain understanding and to humble yourself before your God, your words were heard, and I have come in response to them. But the prince of the Persian kingdom resisted me for 21 days. This was during the time Daniel was fasting and praying, seeking instruction and direction and revelation pertaining to the vision God wanted to show him regarding his people. Your vision will always be for a multitude of people, and not merely for yourself. Also, please note: the position of Daniel's heart was heard the very first day that he humbled himself and sought understanding concerning the vision before any words proceeded from his mouth! This is how I believe that one way or the other, we will write a vision for our lives! Even from the positions of our hearts and the level of humility before God! David the Psalmist wrote: Search me, O God, and know my heart; test me and know my anxious thoughts. See if there is any wicked and offensive way in me, and lead me in the way of everlasting! Psalm 139:23-24. The text goes on to say, Then Michael, one of the Chief Princes came to help me, but I was detained (in the spiritual realm) there with the kings of Persia (evil spirits and powers). This is the epitome and definition of spiritual warfare." Now I have come to explain to you what will happen to your people in the future, for the vision concerns a time yet to come. As you can clearly see, I think that it is important to note here that "delay is not denial." Could what you are waiting for and believing God about be because you are not praying and fasting, perhaps?

Could it be that you are not cognizant of the Fact that there is a battle going on and that those forces that are designed to stop you are assigned to steal, to kill, and to destroy? John

10:10. God withholds "no good thing to them who walk uprightly." Psalm 84:11.

Again, God says: Fear not little flock; for it is your father's good pleasure to give you the kingdom! Luke 12:32. And just in case this is not sufficient, consider the following: and from the time John the Baptist began preaching until now, the kingdom of heaven has been forcefully advancing, and violent people are attacking it! Matthew 11:12.

For those who may not be aware, in Revelation Chapter 12, there was a war recorded in heaven between Satan and Michael, the Archangel of God. In short, Satan, who was created as Lucifer, an angel who was in the very presence of God, thought that he could become God by overthrowing him but was instead cast out. Coincidentally, he influenced a third of the angels who sided with him and was also cast down to the earth with him. So at present, there are no more wars in the realm of heaven where God sits. However, there are 3 levels or divisions of heaven in totality. Let me explain. The third heaven is where God himself sits. Then there is the second heaven where Satan and his demons and angel's rule. This is where he commands from and gives orders to his servants upon the earth. Lastly, the First heaven is where the physical manifestations of heaven are seen with the natural eye, e.g. sun, moon and the stars. From the realm of the second heaven, Satan and his powers try to intercept and hold up what God sends to us as his people from the third heaven. So, he who was cast down to the earth makes war with the seed and children of God and those upon the earth. As a result, the kingdom of God and his people have been "forcefully" advancing, which is the operative word. The violent people that are attacking at present are the fallen angels who inform and inspire spirits of darkness who then attack the people of God. On the contrary, they also empower and inhabit individuals to do their bidding upon the earth. Whether it is the Holy Spirit or an evil Spirit, both desire to inhabit and fill an individual and people for their plans and purposes, and as Satan is a copycat and a thief, he mimics what he has seen and known the father to do and be. This is why there are many, many things that have been reserved for this time and season, including the writing of your individual and unique vision! But thanks be unto God that God rules heaven in totality; period!

So to reiterate Daniel's account, the moment Daniel purposed in his heart and mind to understand the vision, the angel was sent to him "immediately," even before he said a word verbally. However the angel and the answer was detained or delayed. Get the understanding and wisdom!

The angel was sent immediately. However, he did not reach Daniel until 21 days later, although he was sent "immediately." Only at that point was the angel allowed to share with Daniel the vision and what would take place in the future for his people. So is it with the visions that God grants to us. They are already done. We just have to decide whether or not we will wait for the manifestation of what our hearts and minds have spoken life into. For the vision is for an appointed time, wait for it, even though it may tarry, it will surely come!

Whatever is written, my friends, must come to pass! It is not a matter of the authenticity and power of God's word rather whether or not we ever tap into and realize that He has a unique and individualized plan and purpose and vision for each of us. There is not one person that does not have the DNA of God on the inside of them as one who was "made in His likeness and his image. " I don't care who you are, what you believe, what you have done, or if you don't even believe that a God exists! You could be a witch, a warlock, a wizard, a fortune teller, or a consulter of familiar and evil spirits and spirits of the dead! The fact remains that, you too, have been created with the same DNA but have a choice to choose whom you will serve! This was the very purpose that Jesus came to the earth for; "to destroy the works of the devil!"

Write Your Way Out: If Not Now, When?

Therefore, when Christ came into the world, he said: sacrifices and offerings you did not desire, but a body you prepared for me: with burnt offerings and sin offerings, you were not pleased or satisfied. Then I said, "Here I am-it is written about me in the book! I have come to do your will, my God." Hebrews 10:5-9.

Notice that the text says that "Christ came into the world." His purpose for coming was because "sacrifices and offerings" were not sufficient. Things burnt in the fire and offerings made for sins He was not pleased with. So for those who sacrifice and offer children and animals etc., as worship, you are not doing so to God but to demons! Please keep in mind that He always existed. This was even before He came to the earth. This was before He took on a body and became flesh. Then Jesus tells the father that as the written word in flesh, He would come to do what was written of Him in the book. He did this in order to do and complete the will and vision of God for His life, in addition to the plans and goals of His father. It was God's will and vision for a multitude of people, even the world! So is it as it pertains to our visions. The book and vision came to earth and came to pass, manifesting Himself at the appointed time! So again, my friends, whatever is written must come to pass, because what is written is both spirit and life!

Chapter 7
Your Testimony Is The Treasure That Connects You To Your Vision: Reach Back Into Your Treasure Chest

As a clinician in training in the field of counseling, and also as a Community Health Educator, Alcohol and Substance Abuse Counselor in Training, Certified Peer Recovery Advocate, HIV Counselor and Recovery Coach, I am constantly reminded of the importance of helping clients "stay in the present" regarding their mental health and even Drug and Alcohol addictions. Even when it comes to individuals who have been affected by many traumatic experiences, we are trained in "Motivational Interviewing and counseling" and "Cognitive Behavioral Therapy" (CBT) to help them navigate from where they currently are to where they hope and wish to be.

CBT suggests that our thoughts create our emotions, and our emotions create our behaviors and our behaviors our actions. Motivational interviewing does just what it suggests that it does; motivate and encourage individuals to be their best selves. But as good as these techniques are, they are still limited to some degree. Could this be the reason why so many of us are in the present still living to some degree in our pasts? Could this also be the reason why some of our victories in life are so short-lived?

The bible declares that "His thoughts are not our thoughts,

nor is His ways our ways." Clearly, as it relates to the above-stated information, I can see why. First, the word of God declares that we are to, at times, "return to the old landmarks," which is the direct opposite of what society and even we as clinicians believe. In the book of Malachi Chapter 3, God declares to His people, "Return unto me, and I will return unto you," and in the book of Revelation, again, we are urged to "come back to our first love." Nevertheless, I have this against you, that you have left your first love. Remember therefore from where you have fallen; repent and do the first works, or else I will come to you quickly and remove your lamp-stand from its place—unless you repent. (Make a change in mind, heart, & direction). So, if God requires us to "return to Him," it would only suggest to me that He is asking His creation to return back to the Creator and Manufacturer for repair. There are times that we must go back in order to get to the root of our problems, our addictions, to the root of our lust and promiscuities. We must go back to get to the root of our homosexuality and alternative lifestyles in order to get to the root of those things that affect us and our walks in life, and with the one that we say we love and follow; even the one that supplies us with our visions!

As a Personal Testimony, I was born Premature at 4pds 8 oz. So I believe that I have been on the Devil's hit list and a personal assignment of his since "before I came out of my mother's womb." I was raised without my biological dad for much of my childhood and adult years (although I did have a great stepfather), in addition to salvaging the relationship between myself and my biological dad before he passed in 2015. This is something that my brother and I are truly grateful for. What he was unable to do with us because of many years of battling his own demons, he was able to do just that and more for his grandchildren and our children. We actually turned out to be very good friends.

It would turn out that I would also experiment with drugs

at an early age. I also sold drugs and led a promiscuous lifestyle while doing so. Starting out as early as a teenager, at the age of 19 or 20 years old, I had thoughts of suicide and contemplated taking my own life at times. Shortly thereafter, I was introduced to *"witchcraft"* through a relationship in my early years as a young adult. At this point, I walked into a Psychiatric Hospital in the Bronx because of my continued and lingering thoughts of suicide coupled with a concoction of sex, drugs, and rock and roll, which for me was more like, sex, drugs and witchcraft! I remember it as if it was yesterday. As I sat on my bed crying with tears coming down my face, a Hispanic lady with long jet-black hair, who also had on glasses, walked down a long hall toward me that seemed as if it took her an eternity to reach me. She had on her finest "hospital-issued gown." As she made her way to me, the staff called out to her to return in the other direction as if she was out of order or disrupting the normal process of things. But she continued to make her way to me. She sat on the edge of my bed and literally wiped the tears from my eyes, and told me not to take any medications, and I didn't. She assured me that everything would be ok as I shared my story, life, and relationship with her. As slow as it took her to reach me, she got up and made her way in like manner back in the other direction. I was there for about 3 days max. Somebody say, "On the 3rd day!"

For many years I dealt with insecurity and feelings of inadequacy and not being worthy and good enough. This stemmed from some childhood issues but was really strengthened by all of the negative words and voices that I heard from the people closest to me in my late teens and early adult years. If you hear something long enough, you will begin to believe it! But then it all changed! Then I got saved! I remember being out all night and felt the need and urge to go to church that morning, not realizing then that it was the Lord's doing all the time. I remember wearing some shorts, sneakers and a tee shirt. Now anyone knows that you don't go to church on any day in such attire, let alone on a Sunday! Then to make matters worse, this was a "Church of God In Christ," Pentecostal and Holiness Church! Could you imagine?

As I got to the steps of the church, I went to step up to go in, but if anyone is aware of the influence and sway of the evil one, then you know that he is not just willing to let an individual go, who has served him up unto the point of conversion and salvation; so I changed my mind and started walking in the other direction. This yes and no syndrome lasted for about 5 or 10 minutes when God sent a ram in the bush to assist me! The pastor of that church, the shepherd himself, Pastor Percy E Hughes of Bronx Church of God in Christ comes out the door with a bag of garbage in his hand. Of all the people, he comes out with a bag of garbage! If that does not scream, "shepherd," I don't know what else does. I still believe to this day that it was the Lord who sent him out to me. And the rest is history! He ushered me in while service was already going on and ordered them to stop. He then told them of my dilemma and the whole church started to pray for me, and at that moment, I began to cry out to the Lord, and he met me, saved me, and gave me his precious Holy Spirit, and I have been running for my life ever since. God began to show me Himself in his word; literally, He gave me a yearning and desire for the ministry of deliverance and began to speak to and through me prophetically. And the psychiatric hospital that I visited in my early twenties would turn out to be the very place that I would be employed some thirty years later! The very floors that I visited are now the floors that I minister to countless individuals who are in the same place that I once was... "For by the grace of God there go I."

Don't run from your past and your testimony. Rather embrace it! You see, this is what makes you who you are and has a great deal to do with your vision. I like to think that my testimony is not my "all in all, "but rather the stepping-stone and mechanism whereby God allowed me to "reach back into

Write Your Way Out: If Not Now, When?

my treasure chest" and pull out some of the treasure that was buried inside in order to discover who I am in Him, in addition to the next steps, "at best" as a starting point and road map to where He is leading and guiding me.

You see, so many of us run from and abhor the things that we have endured and been through (and rightfully so) because of the many pains and hurts and traumas that are attached to them; however, more times than not, these things are the very mechanisms and conduits whereby the greatest expressions of God's love flows to us and works through us to be a blessing and encouragement to someone else. There is truly a freedom and liberation in knowing and accepting this truth as reality.

Do you really believe that God would allow us to go through seasons of suffering just for suffering's sake? Did He do so with his son? Did He not allow his son to suffer in order that you and I could be reconciled to Him? So is it as it pertains to you and me! Our sufferings are always used for more than just ourselves.

They are used to potentially bless a multitude of people. And with all due respect, God does not lead us down a road of suffering. We lead ourselves down this road oftentimes because of the choices that we have made. But even in this, because God is so good and rich in grace and mercy, he works out "all things," the good, the bad, and the ugly of our lives to form and create His masterpiece in us; if we allow Him to do so. So many of us are looking for "get rich schemes" and have tried everything under the sun to no avail. Could it be that your true treasure and riches are wrapped up in the things that you have gone through? Could it be that God is waiting for you to write that book or start that ministry or domestic violence center for women? Could He be waiting for you to start that homeless shelter or rehab facility for people addicted to drugs and alcohol? Could this be where your true treasures and potential reside?

So the word of the Lord to you today is to "embrace your

testimony" (who you are and what he has brought you out of). Embrace the hurt, the pain, the shame and the fear. Embrace the rape or the molestation, the drug addiction and the promiscuous lifestyle. Now, in no way am I implying that you should embrace the actual thing that has been done to you or against you, for that would be insanity!

But what I am saying is that it was not until I allowed God to show me in His word who I was truly in Him that I stopped allowing these injustices and traumas to dominate and control my life, thinking, and the way that I saw the world and people. Embrace the divorce or even the fact that you may have grown up without a dad. Embrace the traumatic events that may have opened the door to your "alternative lifestyle," including lesbianism, homosexuality or abuse, because if you allow God to intervene, He will use such to be a blessing for someone else who is currently on the road that we may have once traveled. But we must release and relinquish such to Him in order that we can become who He truly created us to be before the foundation of the world! Yes, it will be a great task, but you can do it! You can do all things through Christ who gives you strength! Philippians 4:13.

Listen to how the word of God describes such: Let us give thanks to the God and Father of our Lord Jesus Christ, the merciful Father, and the God from whom all help comes! He helps us in all our troubles, so that we are able to help others who have all kinds of troubles, using the same help that we ourselves have received from God. Just as we have a share in Christ's many sufferings, so also through Christ we share in God's great help. If we suffer, it is for your help and salvation; if we are helped, then you too are helped and given the strength to endure with patience the same sufferings that we also endure. So our hope in you is never shaken; we know that just as you share in our sufferings, you also share in the help we receive. (2 Corinthians 1:3-7). Embrace your testimony! Let go and let God! Allow him to turn your tragedy into a testimony!

You are special, my friend, because to those that He gives "treasures of darkness, and hidden riches in secret places," He does so for the purpose and with the intentions of getting to know Him on a level commensurate with what was given. The only way to receive such treasures and hidden riches is through darkness! But as God is intentional in everything that He does, doing so is always for a greater purpose, plan, and outcome for your life! Look no further! Your testimony is your treasure! Reach back into your treasure chest!

And I will give thee the treasures of darkness, and hidden riches of secret places, that thou mayest know that I, the Lord, which call thee by thy name, am the God of Israel. Is: 45:3 again, notice that we are given the "treasures of darkness" and "hidden riches in secret places" so that we may know Him, and know that unequivocally, that it is He who has called us by name! As I do believe that those treasures of darkness as well as the hidden riches in secret places are actual riches and treasures in every sense of the word because the "wealth of the wicked is laid up for the righteous and the just, I equally believe that these again are also the very things that the enemy has used against us that God turns around for good in order to combat the very same forces over our lives and the lives of others. When you realize that your "testimony is your treasure," then you wouldn't dare change a thing that you have been through, neither do you abhor it but rather embrace it. There is overcoming power in your testimony. The Blood of the Lamb that was shed over two thousand years ago has the power within itself to heal and to deliver; however, when the words of my testimony (what God has done for me and where He has brought me from) comes in agreement and alignment and is coupled with the Blood of the Lamb, this gives me the overcoming wonder-working power of the blood in my life and on my behalf to do and become the impossible! Your testimony is your treasure! Reach back into your treasure chest and pull out some of the riches to who you are and were created to be in Him!

What will you decide?

Healers are spiritual warriors who have found the courage to defeat the darkness of their souls. Awakening and rising from the depths of their deepest fears, like a Phoenix rising from the ashes. Reborn with a wisdom and strength that creates a light that shines bright enough to help, encourage, and inspire others out of their own darkness. – Melanie Koukouris.

Chapter 8
Vision Materialized: New Beginnings

Vision Materialized: New Beginnings
Faith is the substance of things hoped for, and the evidence of things not seen. For by it the elders obtained a good report. Through faith we understand that the worlds were framed by the word of God, so that things which are seen were not made of things which do appear. Hebrews Chapter 11:1-3.

First off, faith is described as a "substance." A substance is something that has shape and a form. It is a thing. Substance is defined as follows: a particular kind of matter with uniform properties including its material, matter, and stuff. It is also defined as the real physical matter of which a person or thing consists of, and which has a tangible, solid presence. So clearly, our faith and what we see and believe has the capacity of becoming a physical manifestation and thing, even a substance. It is the thing and matter and substance of what we see and hope for. In fact, it is the very evidence of things that are not yet seen! Better yet, it is the "real physical matter/substance of which a person or thing consists of that has a tangible or touchable solid presence." My God! My Faith is "the real physical matter."

Next, evidence is the available body of facts or information indicating whether a belief or proposition is true or valid. It is also proof, confirmation, verification, substantiation, corroboration, affirmation, authentication, attestation, documentation, support for, backing for, reinforcement for, and grounds for something being true or valid. It is also defined as: "to be or show evidence of." It is by this kind of faith that we not only "obtain a good report" as did the elders, but we are also able to create and form something that would be made "not by what appears as a result but by what was hoped and believed for! What's my point? The right kind of faith and the things that such produce are already manifested before it actually becomes materialized! If I want to check and measure my faith, I need to compare and contrast the "evidence" that this kind of faith produces. So my vision is created and even materialized at true conception.

Let me explain it to you as the Apostle John describes in the book of revelation Chapter 4:1-2. "After this I looked, and there before me was a door standing open in heaven. And the voice I had first heard speaking to me like a trumpet said, "Come up here, and I will show you what must take place after this." At once (or immediately) I was in the Spirit, and there before me was a throne in heaven with someone sitting on it. Clearly as you can see, John was "immediately" in the spirit as it pertained to the "vision" and things that God wanted to make known to him, as he found himself before the one who "sits on the throne." We are never ushered in or allowed to be in that close of proximity for simply "fairy tales" and to hear another "sermon" but rather to hear Logos and Rhema words and instructions! In this presence, it is not "business as usual."

Next, anytime that God is truly involved in the affairs of man, and in the vision that a man has and embarks upon, it will always initiate and require the man to step way out and farther than he ever would have on his own because, in all

Write Your Way Out: If Not Now, When?

actuality, the vision is Gods! Remember, a true vision is always for a people and a multitude. As a wise visionary in every sense of the word, in the person of Pastor Amos F. Kemper III of Saint Samuel Cathedral Church of God in Christ, who has also been a spiritual father and inspiration to me at present (probably more than he realizes) once decreed and declared that there were some amongst him who was and I quote, "Firestarter's, Igniters, and Activators". Anyone who knows him knows his name to be synonymous with prayer, outreach, evangelism, and having a keen and sharp spirit of discernment. These are some of the very attributes that it takes for us to begin to write our visions and to make them plain. You see, to be a fire-starter or an igniter, and an initiator, suggests that you are embarking upon something that has not been done before. It suggests that many will not know or understand, and truth be told, the carrier of the vision does not understand in totality. He is only made privy to more instruction as he implements what has already been given to him. This word has both confirmed and changed the trajectory of my life. It has strengthened and encouraged me, even more, to "not be normal" and to challenge and break the "status quo." One cannot carry nor implement a vision any other way!

So here is the word of the Lord to you my friends:

"Enlarge the place of your tent, stretch your tent curtains wide, do not hold back; lengthen your cords, strengthen your stakes. For you will spread out to the right and to the left; your descendants will dispossess nations and settle in their desolate cities. Do not be afraid; you will not be put to shame. Do not fear disgrace; you will not be humiliated. You will forget the shame of your youth and remember no more the reproach of your widowhood". (Isaiah 54:2-4 NIV). So the Lord is asking you today: are you a fire-starter, initiator, and igniter? Or are you part of the "status quo"? Whichever category that you fall under will determine and even drive your next steps. One thing that I can tell you personally is this: you cannot be an igniter, initiator or fire-starter and accept the mundane, the mediocre, or the same old thing so help me God! Come hell or high water, you will have to pursue, overtake, and recover all to the Glory of God!

References and Citations

Magiclinkhandwriting.com
Creative Writing (Nurtem.com)
Expository Writing (CourseHero.com)
Descriptive Writing (Readingrockets.org)
Persuasive Writing (Readingrockets.org)
Narrative Writing (Self-Publishingschool.com)
Wikibooks.org (Hebrew Roots / The original foundation/
Laying hands Hebraic) (Umich.edu.) (Hand)
Merriam Webster's Dictionary of the English Word
Google's English Dictionary by Oxford Languages
Dictionary.Cambridge.org
Dictionary.com
The Holy Bible Versions:
KJV, NIV, NCV, CEV, ESV, GNT & AMP

Made in the USA
Middletown, DE
03 January 2023